Book 11

Jungle Fright

Reading Practice

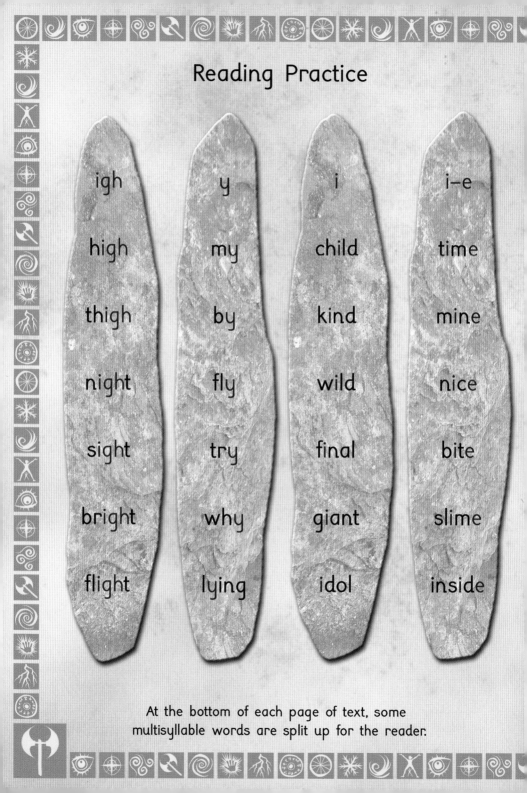

igh	y	i	i-e
high	my	child	time
thigh	by	kind	mine
night	fly	wild	nice
sight	try	final	bite
bright	why	giant	slime
flight	lying	idol	inside

At the bottom of each page of text, some
multisyllable words are split up for the reader.

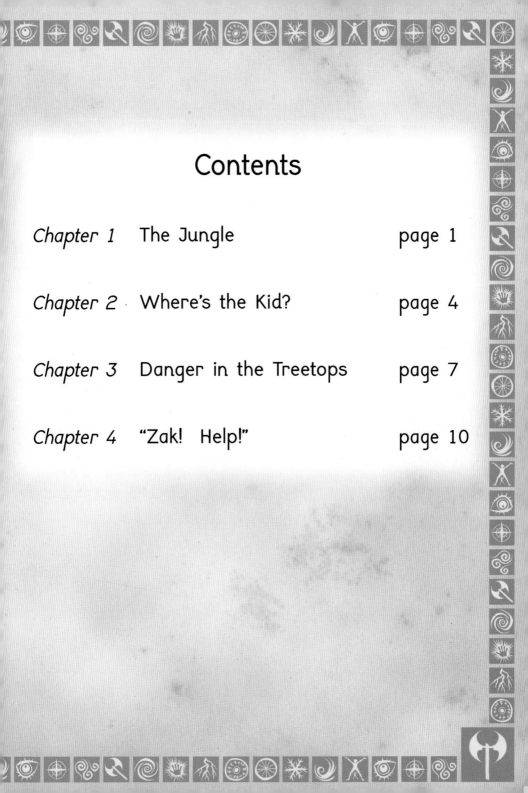

Contents

Vocabulary:

vines   – plants on which grapes grow

beamed down   – sent rays of light

thigh   – the part of the leg above the knee

sloth   – an animal that lives in trees in South America

swipe   – to hit hard with a sweeping blow

tumbling   – falling

Chapter 1
The Jungle

Mim and Zak hiked to a wild jungle. Zak kept looking behind him. A monster might try to follow them...

| jun gle | be hind | foll ow |

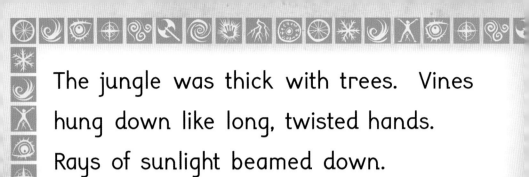

The jungle was thick with trees. Vines hung down like long, twisted hands. Rays of sunlight beamed down.

jun gle   twist ed   sun light

"We might see some parrots fly!" Zak looked up. "We might find spiders that bite," Mim said, looking down.

parr ots   spi ders

Chapter 2
Where's the Kid?

Then there was a cry. Zak and Mim stopped in their tracks. "Where's the kid?" They heard the cry again. "It's the kid!"

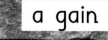
a gain

Mim and Zak ran back. They scanned the branches above them. The bright light blinded them. Then Zak felt something bite him.

bran ches   blind ed   some thing

He looked down and got a terrible fright.

A giant ant was creeping up his thigh.

With a swipe, he sliced it in two.

terr ib le   gi ant   creep ing

Chapter 3
Danger in the Treetops

Zak and Mim looked up. The kid was stranded high up a tree. They climbed higher and higher into the sunlight.

| strand ed | high er | sun light |

Then, a massive hook-like claw swiped at them. It was a giant sloth. It grabbed the kid. Then it swiped at Zak.

mass ive   gi ant

Zak stepped back and fell. He grabbed a branch and held on tight. "Are you alright?" Mim asked. "I'm fine!" he yelled.

al right

Chapter 4
"Zak! Help!"

This time, the sloth took a swipe at Mim. The giant claw landed right beside her. "Zak! Help!" Mim let out a cry.

gi ant   land ed   be side

The staff became a blazing axe. Zak hit the branch with all his might. The sloth and the kid came tumbling down. Mim grabbed the kid as he fell.

bla zing   tum bling

The sloth hit the ground, stunned. "You gave us such a fright!" Mim said to the kid and hugged him tight.